Mastering Bitcoin:

Ultimate Beginner's Guide to Cryptocurrency Technologies - Mining, Investing and Trading in Digital Gold

Matthew Connor

Copyright 2017 by **Matthew Connor** - All rights reserved.

The following eBook is reproduced below with the goal of providing information that is as accurate and reliable as possible. Regardless, purchasing this eBook can be seen as consent to the fact that both the publisher and the author of this book are in no way experts on the topics discussed within and that any recommendations or suggestions that are made herein are for entertainment purposes only. Professionals should be consulted as needed prior to undertaking any of the action endorsed herein.

This declaration is deemed fair and valid by both the American Bar Association and the Committee of Publishers Association and is legally binding throughout the United States.

Furthermore, the transmission, duplication or reproduction of any of the following work including specific information will be considered an illegal act irrespective of if it is done electronically or in print. This extends to creating a secondary or tertiary copy of the work or a recorded copy and is only allowed with express written consent from the Publisher. All additional right reserved.

The information in the following pages is broadly considered to be a truthful and accurate account of facts and as such any inattention, use or misuse of the information in question by the reader will render any resulting actions solely under their purview. There are no scenarios in which the publisher or the original author of this work can be in any fashion deemed liable for any hardship or damages that may befall them after undertaking information described herein.

Additionally, the information in the following pages is intended only for informational purposes and should thus be thought of as universal. As befitting its nature, it is presented without assurance regarding its prolonged validity or interim quality. Trademarks that are mentioned are done without written consent and can in no way be considered an endorsement from the trademark holder.

Table of Contents

Introduction 5
Chapter 1: What is Bitcoin? 7
Chapter 2: Getting Started 10
Chapter 3: Understand the Blockchain and Bitcoin Transaction 16
Chapter 4: Where to Keep Your Bitcoin 20
Chapter 5: How to Buy Bitcoin 23
Chapter 6: How to Use Bitcoin 29
Chapter 7: Investing in Bitcoin 32
Chapter 8: Trading in Bitcoin 36
Chapter 9: Bitcoin for Business 43
Chapter 10: Bitcoin Mining 46
Chapter 11: Bitcoin Security 55
Chapter 12: Other Cryptocurrencies 64
Chapter 13: Tips and Tricks 68
Chapter 14: Bitcoin and Taxes 71
Conclusion 77
One Final Thing… 80
About The Author 81

Introduction

Congratulations on downloading **Mastering Bitcoin – Ultimate Beginner's Guide to Cryptocurrency Technologies - Mining, Investing and Trading in Digital Gold** and thank you for doing so. Cryptocurrency, whether it is Bitcoin or one of the other countless alternatives currently vying for attention, is going to change the world. It isn't a question of if, or even a question of when, it's really just a question of how you are going to capitalize on the fact.

The following chapters will discuss everything you need to know in order to start taking advantage of this burgeoning field successfully. First you will learn all about what Bitcoin is exactly as well as everything you need to know in order to get started on the right foot. Next you will learn about blockchain, the underlying technology of Bitcoin and how a bitcoin transaction works. From there you will learn about where to keep your bitcoins, how to buy them and what you can use them for once you have them in your position.

Matthew Connor

With that out of the way you will then learn about investing and trading bitcoins and how to do each in as profitable manner as possible. You will then learn how it is likely to change small business sooner rather than later. You will then learn how to make money from bitcoins without buying any yourself through the process known as bitcoin mining. You will then learn about the ways you can stay safe when using bitcoin as well as other cryptocurrencies besides bitcoin that you are going to want to keep an eye on. Finally, you will learn some tips and tricks when it comes to interacting with bitcoin as effectively as possible.

There are plenty of books on this subject on the market, thanks again for choosing this one! Every effort was made to ensure it is full of as much useful information as possible, please enjoy!

Chapter 1: What is Bitcoin?

By the fall of 2017, it is unlikely that you haven't heard the term bitcoin at least once or twice. If you still do not know exactly what all the fuss is about, you are not alone because majority of Americans are still fuzzy on the details. The simple answer is that bitcoins are a type of digital money that can be used in all the ways that traditional money can be and more. They are experiencing a massive boom at the moment – thanks to a technology known as *blockchain*.

Theoretical Start

The concept that would eventually help to make blockchains a reality was used for the first time in the 1980s when it was first theorized as a means of preventing spammers from sending out unwanted emails. Known as a proof of work model, the basic idea, and one that is still at the heart of the verification process that blockchain systems use today, is that to send an email the sending computer would need to solve an equation that became infinitely more complicated. Sending one email was easy, sending 10,000 was beyond the power of machines of the time.

This technology more or less lay fallow until the end of the last decade when discussion on a programming forum turned to the possibility of a digital currency that operated like cash in and that it was completely autonomous to use. While most of the programmers in on the conversation were talking about the theory, one programmer who used the name Satoshi Nakamoto was ready to turn the talk into reality. Nakamoto soon released the concept and initial code that would go on to become the investment phenomenon known as *Bitcoin*. Once other developers bit on the open source code, the Nakamoto alias faded into the background, never to be heard again.

To understand blockchain technology more readily, let us consider the way in which bitcoins actually function. In general, they are a type of digital currency that works the same way as any other online payment system. Where the differences come in, however, is the currency that is being traded in these transactions. While all previous types of digital transactions have been completed as a stand-in for analog currency, cryptocurrency transactions exist purely in the digital space.

Each bitcoin gains value based on what is agreed upon by the market as a whole. Transactions that occur are then verified by third-parties before being added to the blockchain directly. This verification is known as bitcoin mining and is done through the use of specialized hardware which is tuned to completed extremely complicated proof of work models as quickly as possible to verify the authenticity and accuracy of each individual transaction. Miners are then rewarded for their service with a small amount of the currency they are mining to offset their costs.

The global exchange rate for bitcoins is known to vary drastically. As if to prove this point, Bitcoin ended the summer of 2017 by dropping more than $1,000 after reaching new highs of more than $5,000 in August. Since its creation, Bitcoin has seen an unsteady, but undeniably strong, upward momentum from its original price of $.02.

2014 marked another exciting development for blockchain technology. Not only was bitcoin worth more than $1,000 for the first time and starting to catch on with mainstream investors in a big way, but it was also when smart contracts were discovered. Perhaps it is more accurate to say that the ability to create smart contracts was created as before that the blockchain was only home to stagnant information. Not so anymore, however, as smart contracts are active code that can be injected into a block to carry out a specific task at a later date. The cryptocurrency platform known as Ethereum has since taken over the smart contract space in a big way. https://www.thebalance.com/how-bitcoins-are-taxed-3192871

Chapter 2: Getting Started

Currently, there are more than 1,000 different cryptocurrencies on the market today. Including bitcoin which accounts for more than 50 percent of the total value, their combined market cap is approximately 60 billion dollars which put them in the same general ballpark as companies like Tesla and Microsoft. With numbers like these, it is easy to see why making the decision to learn more about bitcoin, the king of them all, was clearly the right call.

A cryptocurrency is any type of digital currency that is purely based on computer code and cryptographic processes and relies solely on the market as a means of determining its value. Cryptocurrencies are tracked autonomously through the blockchain they are a part of, and the sphere of influence that investors exert is enough to control it without the need for the governmental oversight that traditional forms of currency required. Bitcoin is the current leader in the space, while Ethereum is the alternative that is currently the closest to challenging its dominance. Despite this fact, many of the lesser known cryptocurrencies offer up a variety of strengths that could make them viable alternatives rather than simple also-rans.

While more traditional currencies are always going to be limited in their growth based on external values, cryptocurrencies generally run the gauntlet from less than a single cent all the way up to nearly $4,000. Broadly speaking, cryptocurrencies can be split into two types, those that are controlled by a centralized source, such as the currency that China recently announced, or those, like bitcoin, that are completely decentralized. The decentralized versions typically require more stringent verification methods to ensure that transactions easily get to where they need to be. Aside from the standard proof-of-work model, consensus protocols or consensus platforms can also be used.

Pricing

While cryptocurrencies do not have their prices controlled by a third party, that does not mean they aren't still bound by the laws of supply and demand. The price of a given cryptocurrency is always going to reflect the value the market assigns to it, which actually makes it a cleaner reflection of the concept than traditional currencies. Likewise, just because there is no guiding hand, does not mean cryptocurrency prices aren't affected by external events. In fact, they are more likely to be affected by a wider array of situations as there is no limit to what might cause investors to sell.

When it comes to primary pricing influences, speculative investors play a much larger role in determining the current price of all cryptocurrencies, especially when compared to more traditional currency types. Cryptocurrency trading works just the same as any other type of trading. Traders purchase a specific cryptocurrency that they hope will do well and then sell it when the opportunity to make a profit presents itself. When enough speculative investors buy into a specific currency and decide to hold, then the result is that a pricing bubble starts to form. As the cryptocurrency market is already extremely speculative in nature, it is particularly prone to this type of phenomena.

Pricing bubbles aren't all bad, however, at least as long as you managed to get in on the investment in question early enough to make a profit from the increasingly unrealistic price a bubble scenario with raise the cryptocurrency to. They are only really unfortunate for those who bought in late and decided to hold when it became clear that things weren't going to be turning around anytime soon.

It is also possible for external forces to combine in such a way that they can drive the price of a given cryptocurrency down, regardless of what the current level of demand might otherwise be. When this scenario occurs, it is not uncommon for the creators of the currency to attempt to take a more active role in the market process in hopes of stopping the downward trends in their tracks.

The first stop when it comes to changing public opinion is to increase the coverage of the cryptocurrency in question in the media. Increased coverage in the media is a great way for outside forces to manipulate the public by ensuring that they have something specific to focus on. Artificially generating public interest then typically leads to an almost immediate increase in price as late-to-the-party investor rush to jump on what they see as the next big thing. Common times for the media to take an interest in a specific cryptocurrency include when it has been added to a new major cryptocurrency exchange, or when one which has been previously featured has a serious new update to its code. Additionally, the media loves a good soundbite or anything that shows the market for cryptocurrency is growing as a whole. Regardless of the context, the more people who hear the name of the cryptocurrency in question, the more the price will ultimately rise.

Having the right type of media coverage will go a long way towards changing the public's opinion about a specific cryptocurrency, but it isn't going to do all of the work. This is mainly going to be done by the main proponents of the cryptocurrency in question. No matter how new a given cryptocurrency is, it is safe to assume that there is a vocal minority online that is willing to tell you why it is the greatest thing since sliced bread. These types of subgroups are often extremely useful when it comes to making moves that are likely to help to artificially inflate the price in question. What's more, this group of users will often work directly with the developers to improve the code for the cryptocurrency in addition to investing their own capital into it directly, all of which helps to increase its price overall.

A clear example of this occurred during the bitcoin bubble of 2014. Bitcoin was just months away from hitting $1,000 for the first time, and traditional investors were starting to take notice. Despite having already been around for five years, bitcoin finally reached the level of mass adoption it required to spread word of mouth like wildfire and suddenly a currency that had previously just been used to buy drugs on the darknet was selling for more than $1,000 per coin.

Another common way these days to generate liquidity, one of the most important things to generating growth in the long-term for cryptocurrencies, is to generate automatic trades that are carried out by bots. This ensures that public interest remains stimulated and helps the price to remain at a steady rate. Liquidity relates to the amount of a given asset that is currently available to trade, and if it is low, then those looking to trade in a specific cryptocurrency will not have any means of purchasing it. As such, when the bots are deployed, their simulated transactions are then enough to often generate additional units of currency, thus improving liquidity overall. This practice is primarily prevalent in China where there are far fewer restrictions on what is and is not allowed in the cryptocurrency market. This has reached such epic proportions that China is actually responsible for a large number of bitcoins overall total liquidity.

Chapter 3: Understand the Blockchain and Bitcoin Transaction

Blockchain technology is likely to come up in conversation when it comes to discussing smart contracts, Ethereum, Bitcoin, or cryptocurrency in general. Regardless of the specifics, the conversation is going to revolve around the fact that blockchain technology is useful when it comes to storing large amounts of primarily financial data in a database that is not accessible in a traditional centralized fashion. Blockchain technology has quickly become known for its extreme combination of security and accessibility.

Each individual block in the blockchain contains numerous different transactions as well as information that marks its unique place in the blockchain as a whole. When new information is added to the version of the blockchain that is connected to a specific node, then that information is automatically transferred to all the other nodes in the system. When information is verified and added to the chain, it automatically receives a timestamp as well, so it is exceedingly easy to determine exactly when each transaction took place.

The auto-sorting nature of blockchain makes it possible for each to operate independently of all external control. Rather than a guiding hand, all of its processes are designed to take place automatically which means a single blockchain could easily be spread around the entire world and operate as if it were located in a single office. The nodes in the system then interact with one another via a means of specifically designed cryptography.

Blockchain technology allows for read access for users who have made transactions as well as write access for nodes. Users who can see but not touch can view their relevant transactions while nodes, and those with access to them, have the power to add new blocks to the chain directly. Blockchain security is so tight that it does not need to worry about actively combating external threats. Instead, its very nature ensures it is as secure as it is possible for a database to be given current technology limits.

Blockchain components

Database: When it comes to the differences between a blockchain database and a traditional database, the primary disparity is how latency is dealt with. With a centralized database, all of the information is kept as close to all the rest as possible to ensure that latency is kept to a minimum.

Decentralized databases, on the other hand, do not care about latency at all, and in giving up on being latency free, they then become unencumbered enough to be spread out across any distance based on user need. With this sort of utilization method in place, blockchain allows the currency to move in the same way that information does online.

Security: The cryptographic security surrounding blockchain is by far its most unique feature. This security comes from its decentralized nature as much as being a part of it. It works based on the self-sorting nature of all of the blocks in the chain. For a new block to be added to the chain successfully, all of the relevant information inside of it is going to have to be verified by all the other currently active nodes that are running the chain at that point and time. A full 51 percent of these nodes are going to have to confirm that the information provided is accurate before it will be accepted into the chain.

While this sounds pretty straightforward, what it means when it comes to cybersecurity is that the only way for false information to make its way into the blockchain is if more than 51 percent of all of the nodes running a particular blockchain would all need to be contaminated with false information at the same time. While it is not outside the realm of possibility for such a setup to occur, the cost and logistical requirements to do such a thing vastly outpace the potential for personal gain.

Relevant information: Each block contains the data that tells the location it maintains in the chain as a whole as well as the relevant transaction data that it was created to house in the first place. The transaction data takes up almost all of the available space so that after it is verified, it moves to the nearest node and into the blockchain proper via a process called the best effort model. This model states that information is moved between relevant nodes based on which would require the smallest expense of additional energy. This is what allows the blockchain to work autonomously without a guiding force.

Verification: Once a new block is added to the chain, it is verified against the prime timeline and then given its proper place in the chain as a whole. After this occurs, the blockchain then logs the block's relevant data and also verifies that its proof of work was completed properly to ensure the block was created in a legitimate fashion. As previously mentioned, these proof of work models require more computational power with each additional transaction that a blockchain contains which is why specialized machines are required to mine successfully.

Chapter 4: Where to Keep Your Bitcoin

Before you will be able to start interacting with bitcoins in a meaningful way, the first thing you will need to do is choose a bitcoin wallet. As your bitcoins are going to have no physical analog or proof of ownership, the wallet that you choose to keep them in is extremely important as it will be the last line of defense between your bitcoins and thieves who want to steal them. While a bitcoin wallet protects your bitcoins, in reality what it is doing is keeping the public and private keys that are connected to your bitcoins safe. If the private key falls into the wrong hands then you will lose all of your bitcoins so it is important to treat these keys the way you would any other valuable commodity.

There are several different types of wallets depending on what you are going to use your bitcoins for and what type of interactions you plan on completing on a regular basis. The most common type of wallet is an online wallet which can be accessed from any device with a web browser, regardless of the type of operating system that it is using. Similar to these are software wallets which store your coins on a specific device rather than on the server of a third party, they often have

Bitcoin

custom interfaces for spending your bitcoins in real world scenarios as well. Both of these options are great if you plan on doing more with your bitcoins than simply hanging on to them and waiting for the price to increase.

If you are primarily interested in keeping your bitcoins secure so that you can cash them in for a profit at a future date them you will likely be more interested in a hardware wallet. This is an encrypted USB drive that comes with its own interface for interacting with your bitcoins when you plug it into a computer. Alternately, you can get a hardware wallet that has its own screen to display relevant information. These types of screens provide extra security because the data displayed doesn't need to touch a potentially malware infected computer at any point.

Last but not least, if you want to keep your bitcoins secure but also would like to be able to easily spend them from time to time then a paper wallet is going to be what you are looking for. A paper wallet is stored on a computer that is not connected to the internet and holds all of your bitcoins. When you want to purchase something with your cryptocurrency you the print out a temporary URL that can be accessed to complete the transaction at the desired time.

In order to get started with bitcoin as quickly and easily as possible you will likely want to start with a service that is simple and easy to set up such as the Coinbase Copay wallet that can be found at CoinBase.com and is available for all major platforms. However, this is just a good place to start as all software wallets are what as known as hot wallets which means that, as they are connected to the internet, which means that there is no way for them to be 100 percent secure. The best way to think of a hot wallet is like the wallet you use on a day to day basis, fine for typical transactions but not nearly secure enough to hold your life savings in.

Chapter 5: How to Buy Bitcoin

Getting started: Assuming you went with the Coinbase option outlined above, the first thing you are going to need to do after downloading the application is to fill in your personal details. Once this is done you will then be taken to your account page which will likely look similar to the online banking software your primary bank uses.

Buying bitcoins with traditional currency: After you have found your wallet of choice and set it up, the easiest way to buy bitcoins through most software wallets is through the program directly. You will likely be able to determine if you wish to use your debit or credit card, or if you would prefer to make a bank transfer. Once the transaction is completed the bitcoins will then be transferred to your wallet. You will not receive a one to one when it comes to the amount of USD you put into the system as there will be varying fees associated with the transaction as well. Which payment methods are going to be available will vary based on where the exchange was incorporated. Again, most systems are relatively straightforward and you should be able to proceed by just clicking the "buy" tab in most instances. The same goes for selling when the time comes to do so.

Regardless, you will need to give out your credit card or bank information which means that it is important that you do your due diligence beforehand and make sure the place you buy your bitcoins from is trustworthy. The way these types of services work is that a particular exchange is affiliated with one or more different wallets. When you are agreeing to buy bitcoins through your wallet what you are really doing is buying through that exchange which means that there still needs to be someone willing to sell waiting on the other side. In general, these companies do not recommend storing a large number of bitcoins in their system for a prolonged period of time.

Picking an exchange

If you are using a wallet that is not connected to an exchange directly, then this means you will need to choose one yourself, which can be easier said than done. One great thing about the bitcoin market is that the exchanges never sleep. It does not matter the time or the place, you can log on to an exchange and trade bitcoin with someone somewhere in the world. This is due to the fact that there are over 100 different exchanges around the world, all offering different currency pair and different rates, making it practically impossible to not find one that fits your particular needs and investment goals. This, coupled with the fact that virtually anything can set off a trend in either direction means that swings of five percent or greater are common with bitcoin and smaller exchanges can see changes of upwards of 20 percent in a single day.

Volatility like this is the reason it is so important to find an exchange that you can trust, as there is too much chance in the market already to add yet another thing to the list. As such, the first thing you are going to want to do when it comes to choosing an exchange is as much research as you can on the company itself and all its ins and outs. If you skip this step, then you could conceivably end up in a scenario where your exchange closes up shop and takes your money with it in the process. If this occurs, then it is unlikely that you are going to have much in the way or recourse which is why it is so important to choose wisely in the first place.

One of the most important traits for your bitcoin exchange to have is the level of transparency the exchange holds itself to for its day to day operations. This means you are going to want to take a look at their order book and also be provided with details such as where the company holds its funds and how their levels of reserve currency are verified. If these sorts of things are not readily available, and the company isn't extremely new, then there is likely a reason they prefer for this not to be the case. While this will not always be the case, exchanges that do not make all of their details public have the potential to be fractional exchanges which means they do not keep enough money on hand to satisfy all their debts to their clients at once. As such, if there was ever a reason everyone needed their money back at once, the exchange would run out of money and default. It should go without saying that fractional exchanges should be avoided at all costs.

Assuming their details are acceptable, the next thing you are going to want to research is the type of security that the exchange is utilizing when it comes to keeping your money safe. This means you are going to want to ensure that the site is running a secure HTTPS as opposed to the more common HTTP. Additionally, it is important that in addition to requiring that you enter a password, they require that you utilize some form of dual-factor authentication. If you end up choosing an exchange with less than this level of security, then all you are doing is putting your investment currency at risk.

As with their going rates for different cryptocurrencies, each exchange is going to have varying rates and fees associated with having an account with them. The amount that you are going to have to pay to have a transaction verified on the blockchain is going to stay the same, but what you are going to have the pay the exchange is going to vary based on either a flat per transaction rate or based on a portion of the transaction that was completed. This is not the case in China, however, where there are no exchange fees outside of what the blockchain charges to verify the transaction. Especially if you are trading on a regular basis, these fees can add up extremely quickly which means it is important to know what you are getting yourself into before you make a more official commitment.

In addition to the cost of each transaction, it is important to have a clear idea of just how long it is going to take between when you place your order and when it is going to be completed. A longer transaction time isn't inherently inferior to a longer one, as long as the exchange handles the delay in the right way. Specifically, it is important to ensure that your price is locked in when the transaction is placed, not when it is completed. If this is not the case, then you could end up paying a dramatically different price depending on how long the transaction takes to process.

Finally, it is important to try and find a local exchange whenever possible. First and foremost, choosing an exchange in your own country dramatically increases the odds that, if your exchange does vanish, you will have some level of recourse. This is still far from a sure thing, however, but it is better than nothing. Furthermore, using a local exchange will make it easier for you to trade during peak times without having to get up in the middle of the night to do so. A word of warning, however,

Matthew Connor

just because an exchange is in a given country does not mean that it will take your native currency, double check before you make any commitments to save yourself an additional step every time you go to trade.

Chapter 6: How to Use Bitcoin

Before you can use your bitcoins for anything, you will need to create a public bitcoin address which should be easily done through the interface for your bitcoin wallet. This address will be one that you can share with anyone and can be used to add bitcoins to your account. A public bitcoin address is a long string of random letters and numbers that looks like this:

16BPS8xb5k36MeNLWmfZ1zpjCqbDhgyaHg.

Once this address is created you will want to be sure to send a small amount of bitcoin to yourself to test that it works properly. It will likely take between 10 and 20 minutes for the transaction to process but assuming you set everything up properly you will then see the amount reappear in your wallet. You can then give that address out to receive bitcoins for good or services. To pay someone else using your bitcoin wallet all you then need to do is enter their address into your wallet and follow the onscreen instructions.

Using your bitcoins

Once you have some bitcoins in your possession, it is only natural that you want to spend them on something, even if you purchased them primarily for investment purposes. Luckily, there are a wide variety of things that you can do with your bitcoins besides letting them accrue in value.

Utilize bitcoin ATMs: One of the great things about a cryptocurrency investment is that any time you want to turn your investment back into cash, all you have to do is sell part of a bitcoin for its current USD rate. While the same might be said for other types of investments, bitcoin is the only type of security that allows you to take small portions of your investment out of the bank in $20 increments. Currently there are more than 2,000 bitcoin ATMs across the United States alone with similar numbers popping up around Europe and nearly 3 times that number in China alone. These ATMs typically charge anywhere between 5 and 8 percent of the total transaction. Check out CoinATMRadar.com to see where the closest bitcoin ATM is to you.

Utilize OpenBazaar.org: Open Bazaar is an online auction house, much like eBay. Buyers and sellers aren't required to pay any fees outside of what is normally required for a bitcoin transaction and signing up is free. What's more, as the price is often set in bitcoin it is possible to keep an eye on the price and wait for drops before swooping in and picking up items cheap before their prices have time to be adjusted. If you are interested in building up your supply of bitcoins but don't have a lot of capital to put into the endeavor up front then sites like OpenBazaar.org are a great place to start.

Trade cash for bitcoin or bitcoin for goods and services: While trading online for bitcoin outside of an approved exchange is not recommended, trading bitcoin out in the real world is an extremely safe proposition. If you are looking to buy your bitcoins in the real world then you can use LocalBitcoins.com to find a local dealer in your area. In this scenario you would hand the dealer your cash and they would send the bitcoins to your wallet while you wait to ensure you are avoiding fraud. If you are looking to trade your bitcoins for goods or services, all you need to do is keep an eye out in the real world as every day more and more businesses are starting to accept bitcoin as a viable alternative to cash.

Chapter 7: Investing in Bitcoin

Investing in bitcoin is extremely similar to investing in any other type of commodity except that the potential for return manifests itself in sometimes as little as a few weeks rather than months or years. Nevertheless, the core goal is going to remain the same, find a way to allow your money to work smarter rather than harder. Due to the volatile nature of bitcoin, you are likely to make as much on a major move by adopting a buy and hold strategy as you would sitting in front of your computer every day and making much smaller trades. This significantly skews the effectiveness of short-term trading while improving the odds on long-term trading while also providing it with some additional options.

The biggest of these is what is known as compounding, which is the idea that it is important to reinvest as much of your early profits as possible back into the initial investment as a means of maximizing your long-term results. Reinvesting both early and regularly is crucial to maximizing your profits in the long-term and the longer you have to let the profits build upon themselves the more powerful the force of compounding will be.

To understand the true potential of compounding, consider a college student with a fresh master's degree in hand and 40 years to go until retirement. If they want to be a millionaire by the time they retire all they need to do is to save $900 per month and ensure that their investments generate an average 5 percent return on investment each year (or what bitcoin can see in a matter of hours). However, if that same person waited 10 years to get started they would need to save $2,000 per month to hit the same goal. Meanwhile, if they waited 20 years then they would need to save more than $4,000 a month to be at the same place when retirement came knocking.

Aside from getting started as quickly as possible, it is important to understand your personal investment habits in order to ensure that your personal habits are helping, rather than hindering your investments. No strategy is going to be right for everyone and in order to start cutting some from the stack the first thing you will need to do is to consider how comfortable you are with risk. As bitcoin is naturally a risky proposition, you will obviously going to be at least partially amiable to risk, but there is still a wide degree of variance to choose from.

It will also be important to consider your goals when it comes to investing as these can easily affect the ultimate strategy that you choose to pursue. This could be something safe, such as keeping your initial investment intact no matter what, or it could be something with a greater amount of risk and potential reward. The specifics themselves don't matter, what matters is that you take the time to clearly identify your plan and then stick with it once it has been instigated. When choosing your goals keep in mind that your investment plans don't exist in a vacuum, be sure to accurately consider any external factors when in the planning stage.

It is also important to seriously consider the amount of money that you would be willing to lose if things ended up not going according to plan. It is important to be honest with yourself about this amount and never invest more than that at once. If you do, you will find that you spend more time worrying about if you are going to lose the money than what you can do in order to ensure that your investment is as successful as possible. Keep in mind that risk and profit are intertwined and that you literally can't have one without the other in equal measure. If you have at least 20 years of prime investing years ahead of you then you will want to take more risks than those who may find themselves somewhat closer to retirement.

Finally, in addition to understanding the potential risk, it is also important to consider how much time you want to spend directly interacting with your trades. If you like the idea of regularly buying and selling in an effort to squeeze the most out of every bit of movement possible then you will want to try trading. Otherwise, the more relaxed pace of the buy and hold strategy will likely suit you better.

Chapter 8: Trading in Bitcoin

2016 was a banner year when it came to the capitalization of cryptocurrencies and 2017 has thus far proven to be even more attractive to investors as far as cryptocurrencies are concerned. Bitcoin showed an increase of greater than 300 percent during this timeframe, ensuring its spot as the reigning cryptocurrency king remains unchallenged. This is not to say that investing in bitcoin is going to be the right choice for everyone, however, and as such, it is important to understand the various pros and cons of this investment opportunity before you commit to anything too enthusiastically.

The biggest pro comes in the added security that your personal information will experience when dealing with bitcoin exchanges compared to traditional exchanges. Not only do you have the inherent security of blockchain technology keeping your personal details safe, in many instances, you will not be required to divulge any personal information to get started trading bitcoin, especially if you already have some on hand to begin trading with. When you compare this type of operating setup to a traditional exchange, every single time that a transaction is made is another opportunity for someone to steal protected information.

This isn't even taking into consideration the ways in which digital currency is safer than physical currency. There is no way to forge a bitcoin or generate counterfeit dogecoins and once both parties have committed to a transaction, there is no way that it will not go through as it is impossible to negate a transaction once it has been completed.

The other biggest benefit that bitcoin offers the world is the fact it means that anyone has access to traditional banking services. While this might not seem like that big of a deal to those where such things are commonplace, the fact of the matter is that nearly 50 percent of the world's population still does not have access to these types of services which means that once bitcoin becomes more commonplace it is going to make a serious difference in countless lives. As such, over the next five years, experts anticipate not just an increase in the everyday use of bitcoin, they anticipate a substantial increase. To understand just how significant the change is going to be, consider the fact that more people in Kenya right now have access to a bitcoin wallet than having access to sanitized drinking water.

Another reason that those in underdeveloped portions of the world are flocking to bitcoin is due to the fact that, despite the transaction fees involved, each bitcoin transaction frequently costs less than processing that same transaction through a traditional banking establishment. The same can be said about trades made via bitcoin exchanges which are often times as much as 50 percent cheaper than more traditional exchanges.

Everything is not all sunshine and roses with bitcoin technology, however, at least not yet. The biggest reason that this is the case is due to the fact that the technology surrounding blockchain and bitcoin, in general, is still so knew that it is literally impossible to determine just how it is all likely to shake out. For example, prior to 2014, the idea of smart contracts had never been seriously considered, but now, they are at the forefront of potentially useful blockchain adjacent technology. This means that while there are clearly already profits to be made, the potential for loss is literally unlimited until things begin to stabilize into a more long-term market.

This extreme level of uncertainty translates into a greater than average degree of volatility for all types of bitcoin. In fact, bitcoins are currently considered to be about three times more volatile than gold and four times more volatile than investments in the stocks of the S&P 500. As many early investors have learned, this high degree of volatility can directly translate into serious wins, but it can also translate into significant losses as well. Also affecting all bitcoin prices is the speculative bubble that they exist in. Currently, more than 75 percent of all bitcoin transactions are made for speculative purposes which means the bubble is bound to pop eventually. Only once bitcoin are really being used for their intended purposes will the fear of bubbles become unfounded.

While the digital nature of bitcoin is often touted as a positive, it is important to consider its negative aspects as well. For example, as a purely digital construct, if you were keeping your bitcoin in an exchange that had a server error that resulted in a loss of all its backup drives, what would happen to your currency then? Likewise, what were to happen if you put your coins in a physical wallet that then stopped reading in your computer? Both of these cases are unlikely to happen, but if they were, then your bitcoin would be gone as if it had never existed in the first place. Furthermore, the massive potential for profits means that hackers are never going to stop trying to access these exchanges, so eventually, they are going to succeed. When investing in bitcoin, it is important to value security as highly as possible because there is very little standing between your investments and the void.

Matthew Connor

Making a good trade

In addition to being a potentially lucrative market, trading in bitcoin is a great choice for those who haven't spent much time trading previously because it differs from the standard method in several important ways. The first of these is that there are very few barriers to entry, getting started is as easy as finding an exchange you are interested in and trading your base currency for some bitcoin. Unlike the more unified traditional markets, each bitcoin exchange is independently owned which means the market is extremely fragmented. This leads to larger spreads.

The lack of regulations around these organizations also means that the level of margin that you will be able to trade under is going to be larger than you can get just about anywhere else. Margin can lead to insurmountable losses, however, so it is important to avoid using it until you are very comfortable with the results you have been generating thus far. It is also worth pointing out that the prices for each exchange are going to vary somewhat based on personal supply which means that it is possible to find a bitcoin from one exchange and sell it for a profit on another back to back.

When it comes to trading bitcoin via a trading company, traders use what is known as a contract for difference. In this type of agreement, the seller and the buyer agree to a specific period of time. Once the timeframe expires, the buyer then pays the seller the difference between what the price was at originally, and the price now. If the difference is negative, then the seller pays the buyer instead.

Exchanges to keep in mind

Bitstamp: This cryptocurrency exchange has been around longer than most others on the market today and was first started all the way back in 2011. It is the second most populated exchange and sees more than 10,000 units of currency move each day.

Bitfinex: The most commonly used exchange by a fair margin, Bitfinex moves more than 200,000 units of currency every single week. What's more, they offer new users who come in with cryptocurrency in hand the ability to start trading without any additional verification.

OKCoin: This is a Chinese coin that deals primarily in USD. This, as astute readers will remember, provides a wide variety of unique opportunities to USD holders who are looking for a few less rules standing between them and their trading.

Matthew Connor

Coinbase: This exchange has been operating continuously since 2010 which makes it the oldest continuously active exchange in the world. It is known for being extremely well regulated and even after all this time is still in the top five when it comes to average daily volume.

Chapter 9: Bitcoin for Business

Enhanced efficiency of operations: Businesses have long had a contentious relationship with the traditional financial establishment as the cost of doing business often makes it difficult to live with the banks and impossible to live without them. This can all change with the widespread use of bitcoin technology as blockchain technology features not only better fees, real-time access to money operations and an extremely secure system besides. Additionally, the technology will make it easier for companies to expand in a global economy as a bitcoin is a bitcoin no matter where the buyer lives.

Distributed ledger: The biggest benefit to small businesses is the distributed ledger aspect of the bitcoin blockchain. The data that they need isn't controlled by some third party, it is freely available to everyone on the network when anyone is free to verify all of the transactions that came into and went out of their wallet. Each user will also remain in complete control of their own data which means there is no easy way for cyberattacks to gain access to large amounts of data at once.

When a bitcoin transaction is processed, the fee that is charged is split between the miners and Bitcoin to pay for blockchain maintenance. Despite having to pay out two separate individuals, Bitcoin's fees are still significantly lower than what small businesses offer pay for inferior services from more traditional establishments. When the number of transactions that the average small business does in a month is considered, the savings found by switching to bitcoin can be substantial.

Streamlines practices: Another thing that makes the bitcoin blockchain so useful to small businesses is the number of ways it can streamline common business practices. The process of clearing or settling bank transactions can take days, if not weeks, via traditional methods. This process is as simple as waiting for the block containing your transaction to be verified, something that will generally take about 20 minutes.

With smart contract technology thrown into the equation the potential for streamlining successfully is magnified even further. While some of the more elaborate means of taking advantage of the bitcoin blockchain are likely to be out of the price range of the average small business, the costs of these endeavors will continue to decrease as they become more mainstream. All told, it is likely that small businesses will find smart contract and blockchain technology to make a host of common tasks more manageable while also ensuring they end up cheaper as well.

Chapter 10: Bitcoin Mining

If trading or investing in bitcoin does not sound like it is going to be for you but you still want to make money off this whole bitcoin thing sooner rather than later, then bitcoin mining might be more your speed. In exchange for mining, miners receive a predetermined amount of bitcoin for their help which goes to offsetting costs and also making the entire process worth your time.

The greater the processing power of the machine you use, which is measured in terms of hashes per second, the more likely you will be to complete proof of work models, and the more you stand to make as a result. The most commonly used proof of work model is known as the hashcash model which is a type of cryptographic algorithm which utilizes a hash function at its core. Hashcash proofs can then be set to a specific difficulty to ensure that blocks are not created faster than the blockchain can handle which means it needs to be set based on the number of transactions that can be successfully processed per second. For example, a new bitcoin block is only created every 10 minutes. The probability of successful generation is quite low, so it is practically impossible to determine when a specific machine will generate a new block.

Get into the mining game

The best mining machine and the best price that you can expect to pay for it is something that changes regularly which means that some additional research is going to be required to determine what is currently state of the art. The best place to find out new up-to-the-moment information is going to be on the subreddit for the currency you are considering mining. Once you know what you are looking for, odds are you will be able to find a version of it on Amazon.com.

While the specifics of the system you end up with are going to vary based on the times, one thing that is never going to change is that you will need dedicated hardware to mine bitcoin effectively. While it is technically still possible to mine with a computer's video card or a laptop's CPU, the speed with which modern mining machines can complete proof of work transactions means that you would be unlikely to finish a single verification in a year's time.

ASIC is the company that is known to produce the best products and tends to offer speeds that are roughly a hundred times more than what the average computer can manage. In general, trying to mine without specialized software is going to end up costing you more in electricity than you will end up making on the endeavor. As of fall 2017, the average mining machine costs between $500 and $4,000 with pricier machines resulting in a higher payout.

Once you have a machine in hand, the next thing you are going to need to do is to download the relevant mining software. There are numerous different versions of this software available, and not all are compatible with all types of systems, so it pays to look into the specifics before committing to anything. The most popular versions of the software include CGminer and BFGminer, or EasyMiner for those who aren't comfortable running software from the command line.

Once you have the required software in place, the next thing you will need to do is find a mining pool to join so that you can maximize your potential mining power. A mining pool is a collection of miners that have joined together to ensure that they can mining as many blocks as possible. Like owning a dedicated mining machine, joining a mining pool is technically optional, though the complexity of the average proof of work model is such that joining is really the best way to make in money off the process. When working with a mining pool, you will receive a portion of the profits from every block that your machine helps to verify as determined by one of several different compensation models.

Bitcoin

If you do decide to set out on your own, you will need to download the core client from Bitcoin.com as it is required to ensure your version of the blockchain is synced up with the blockchain prime. If you are planning on joining a pool instead, then all you need to do is ensure that you follow any instructions that the pool sends your way and do your best to keep your behavior in line with any guidelines.

There are a wide variety of different types of mining pools in the validation space these days which can make finding the right one for you something of a chore. To simplify the process as much as possible, the first thing that you are going to want to do is to research the pools you are considering on the relevant subreddit. Doing so will ensure that you can read about each of the pools before you commit to anything and prevent you from signing on with a lemon. While joining a popular pool will often mean you are eligible for more blocks, the amount you get from each will be lower than if you choose a smaller pool. It is typically considered to be better for the health of a particular blockchain if users mine in larger numbers of smaller pools to guarantee that enough proofs are always being generated.

When looking into various pools, you will need to look carefully at any content provided when it comes to how payment is generated as this is a much more complicated process than it may initially appear. There are countless different payment methods, and you would do well to be familiar with the most frequently used varieties to ensure you do not end up with something that you will not like in the long-term.

Pay per share: The pay per share (PPS) model pays miners for their share of the work as soon as the block has been verified with a specific amount for each portion of the proof that their machine generated. Miners are paid out for their work from the pool's total holdings, without waiting for the payment to be processed by the blockchain. This structure is preferred by miner's as it ensures there is very little variance in what each block will generate in profits and it puts all the risk in case something goes wrong onto the pool operator. As there is always a risk that a block will not payout and will instead be orphaned, the operator then runs the risk of not being paid for the work in the long run after having already paid the miners out from the pool's funds. Additionally, the operator is required to have a lot of excess capital on hand to ensure that they can continue to remain solvent during slow periods. Due to these reasons, the PPS model is not as common as it once was.

Proportional approach: The proportional mining approach distributes mining rewards based on the portion of the block that their machine provided. Payments are then generated after payments have been generated for the block in question.

Pay per last N share: The pay per last N Share (PPLN) model is similar to the proportional method except instead of true shares it generates profit margins based on N shares. The difference between it and a PPS model is that an N share pays out a variable rate based on how much was rewarded from the block in question which means the amount each miner receives is always going to vary based on the results. Payments are then sent out after the reward for the block have been received.

Double geometric: The double geometric payment method is a type of hybrid approach to mining payments that splits the risk between the pool operator and the miners. The pool operator then takes a portion of the profits when things are going well and uses those funds to pay miners when things aren't going according to plan. Payments made through this system are generated based on shares and payments are made once a block is successfully added to the chain.

Shared maximum pay share: The shared maximum pay share model (SMPPS) is an updated version of the PPS model that sees more use these days because of the way it mitigates risk for the pool operator. It offers up a reward per share amount that is based on how much the pool has earned in the recent past. Payments are made on a predetermined schedule assuming all relevant blocks have been accepted into the chain.

Recently shared maximum: The recently shared maximum pay per share model (RSMPSS) is another variation on the PPS model that prioritizes newer pool members, so they are more likely to receive a greater number of shares compared to those who have been in the pool the longest. Payments are made at set intervals after all the verified blocks have been successfully added to the chain.

Capped pay per share and back pay: The capped pay per share with recent back pay model of payment (CPPSRB) is a variation of the standard MPPS payment method that pays miners as much as possible based on the rewards generated while ensuring that the pool remains solvent first and foremost. Payments are then sent out after the reward for the block have been received.

Pooled mining model: The pooled mining model (PMM), more commonly known as the slush pool, is a type of payment model where the final shares of a given proof of work model are given a better rate when compared to earlier shares which are naturally easier to generate. This payment model is especially effective when it comes to stopping miners from dropping out of a job after the halfway point when the rewards are fewer compared to the work that is being completed. Payments are then sent out after the reward for the block have been received.

Pay on target: The pay on target (POT) payment method is yet another PPS variation except that this one pays out individual miners based on the resources each one used to generate the proof of work model as a whole. Payment are then only generated on a set schedule after the relevant blocks have all been verified.

SCORE: The SCORE payment model uses a specialized reward system that weighs shares differently based on how quickly the block was mined overall. It also pays more for later shares of any block to compensate for the additional resources required to complete it successfully. Payments are then generated based on the scores that each miner received during the proof. Payments are sent out after the reward for the block have been received.

Eligius: The eligius model of payment was created by the owner of BFG miner in an effort to improve upon the standard PPS model. It uses the strengths of the PPS model along with those of the BPM model to create a payment model that allows miners to be paid for their work right away. Each miner is paid out based on an equation that takes the total reward for a given block and then divides the amount evenly by all the shares that were used to generate the block, while also calculating any users who have shares of stale blocks in the current proof as well. Miners who end up with a stale block then have those shares rolled over into the next successfully completed block they are a part of.

Chapter 11: Bitcoin Security

As with any new technology, the bitcoin market is rife with individuals who are looking to do nothing more than take you for all you are worth. Most people who fall victim to scammers are ignorant of the dangers they faced, so simply by reading this chapter, you will already be significantly better off than you would otherwise be. This does not mean you are going to be well-protected forever, however, as fraudsters are always working on new and improved ways to separate the uninformed from their wallets. As a general rule of thumb, you are never going to want to do business with a bitcoin company that does not have a well-defined reputation, doing otherwise will only put your money at risk.

First and foremost, you are going to need to be on the lookout for entirely fake exchanges. While exchanges are going to have various levels of success when it comes to providing service to consumers, those of this variety do not even make an effort at actual service and instead take the money and run. With a little practice, one look at the advertisements for a given bitcoin exchange will be all you need to determine if it is remotely worth your time. Simply put, if an exchange offers to sell you a specific number of bitcoin for a specific rate, regardless of the current market value, then you can be certain they are a scam.

Bitcoin exchanges work exactly the same as more traditional exchanges which means that for you to buy at a rate that is below market value, someone else would need to be willing to sell for that price which isn't going to happen, that's why it's called market value. When you see this sort of advertisement without any qualifications attached, then you can be sure they are going to ask for you to send your money somewhere and then the promised bitcoins will never materialize. Think of it as a waving red flag and walk the other way.

The other potential scam you need to be wary of that is of a similar sort is phony exchanges that offer to buy your bitcoin through PayPal. Again, this is not the way that standard exchanges operated. If you put money into a given exchange, then that money stays in your account until the bitcoin is transferred, nor are things any different if you are selling bitcoin instead of buying. These sorts of scams then ask for your PayPal details, as if they need them, and the give you a QR code to scan for a link to send your bitcoin to. As in the previous scenario, the promised payment will never arrive. Legitimate exchanges do not use PayPal and generally require extensive verification if you are not trading purely in bitcoin.

Bitcoin

Outside of fake exchanges, you are also likely to come across fake wallets from time to time. These can be more difficult to spot from afar as the scam here typically involves downloading spyware onto your computer that can then be used to harvest valuable personal information, and the program may even otherwise work as promised. The best way to avoid this type of scam is to only stick to the wallets that Bitcoin recommends.

Even then, before you download anything, it is important to use your instincts to determine if anything about the website in question seems not quite right. You will also want to ensure that the URL for the site includes HTTPS, not HTTP. Before you download anything, you will also need to verify that you entered the URL correctly as not doing so can lead to fraudulent sites with similar addresses.

Before you open any files that you have downloaded, you are also going to want to ensure that you scan them to guarantee they are virus free. If you do not have virus software on your computer, you can use the site VirusTotal.com to check it for you. If you are thinking about using a wallet that is not recommended directly by Bitcoin, then the next best option is going to seeing what the community thinks about it on Reddit first. Above all else it is important to not put your faith in a wallet that you do not know is going to be secure, it is literally the only thing standing between your cryptocurrency and nothingness.

Another important type of scam to be aware of is phishing scams. These types of scams require the scammer to convince you that they are some affiliated with either the exchange that you use or even Bitcoin directly. They then either send you to a fraudulent website or give you a phone number to call to hand over all of your sweet, sweet, personal information. Typically contact is made via email, though popup adds are also sometimes used. Regardless, the end result is going to be something that is sure to ruin your day.

If you find yourself with an email that does not seem quite right, the most important thing to do is avoid doing whatever it is that the email is requesting of you. This is obviously easier said than done, especially when the email looks pretty much on the level. The email itself might even be from a legitimate source that was just hacked to give the spammer access to the relevant email accounts.

If this is the case, then the first place you are going to want to look to learn the truth is in any URLs that might be included in the link. While the name of the link can be changed, the URL cannot which means if you hover your mouse cursor over it then you will see where it is really sending you. If you

Bitcoin

ever feel as though you are unsure if you follow the advice in an official sounding email, the best thing you can do is to contact the company that supposedly contacted you directly, via channels that you initiate. This removes 100 percent of the guesswork from the equation, and if the email really is legitimate, it will ensure you get the relevant information as well.

If you find yourself dealing with a lot of phony online advertisements, then the easiest way to reduce their frequency is to take more care when determining what sites you visit online. The most common way many people are introduced to phishing scams is by searching for something related to bitcoin online and then clicking the first link that comes up in the results. The reality is that the first few results have always been paid advertisements which means you are getting nothing from those sites save additional advertisements and opportunities for malware to end up on your computer. You can mitigate this type of risk entirely by simply knowing the URLs you are looking for before you go online.

Another, common bitcoin phishing scam is what is known as the Ponzi scam. The exact specifics of this type of scam will likely vary, but the one thing they will all have in common is that they will offer to take your bitcoin in exchange for an amazing unit price that cannot be beat. The easiest way to avoid this type of scam is to remember that if something appears too good to be true, then it almost always is. If the deal does not give them away, the best way to pick out a Ponzi scam is based on the fact that it works based on a referral process. If you find yourself on a site that is offering you a commission for bringing in other new clients, then you are safe in assuming it is a Ponzi scam. Likewise, if you came across the link to the site at the bottom of some forum post, you probably shouldn't assume it is on the level. Overall, if you are unsure as to the legitimacy of the program in question, then you are going to want to turn to Reddit once more to do some research and again, never trade bitcoin outside of approved channels.

Finally, there is a fair amount of potential for fraudulent practices surrounding mining pools as well. These can also be difficult to determine with complete accuracy as it can be difficult to tell when regular payments for work completed stop and fraudulent payments begin. First things first, a fake mining pool is going to have an initial signup cost, which a real mining pool may or may not have. Once you sign up, you will receive payment for blocks that you have allegedly had a part in mining and things will seem fine. Over time, the payments will slow and then stop altogether as the community, as a whole, catches on to just what is happening.

The best way to avoid these types of scenarios is to, again, be on the lookout for referral services and, above all else, trust your instincts. You will also want to look into all the specifics surrounding the mining pool before you commit to anything. If the pool is new, then there might not be much information available, but if they have been around for a while then the relevant subreddit should have all of the information you need. Furthermore, you are always going to want to remain on the lookout for certain details that a legitimate mining pool will be able to provide.

This includes things like the pool that they regularly mine from as well as the ability to determine which pool your hash rate will be going to. The pool should also have strict limits when it comes to the amount of maximum hash rate they can utilize at one time as adding infrastructure is an expensive and time-consuming process. If you come across a pool that is offering unlimited amounts, then you can be almost certain that they are just scamming miners.

Knowing the right lies to tell is one thing, being able to provide proof of the hardware that the mining pool is working with is another. As such, you should always ask to see pictures of the data center that the mining pool operates out of as well as any other hardware they are currently running. While a scammer might say otherwise, this is actually an extremely reasonable response and only shows that you are being careful about committing your resources. If you get any type of response other than the pictures you requested, then you will know with certainty that you are dealing with a scam.

You are going to also want to keep an eye out for mining pools that have an official endorsement from a vendor of ASIC products. ASIC makes a majority of the equipment that mining pools use so finding a pool that does not use their products or claims to not use their products is enough to be a red flag in and of itself. Likewise, ASIC is always willing to give out a certified logo or an official statement of quality as it helps to reinforce their brand and weed out false competition. If you run across a mining pool that claims to be legitimate but cannot provide this basic information, then you are going to need to think twice about whether it is worth it to take the risk.

When you are still making money as part of one of these fake mining pools, this type of scan will likely seem fairly harmless, after all, you'll still be seeing regular payments. It is still a scam, however, which means that unlike with a traditional mining pool where you can count on payments for work that has actually been done, the amount that you end up making is going to decrease over time as the scam dries up and the scammer prepares to move on to greener pastures. You will be able to determine if you are accidentally affiliated with this type of setup if you start receiving emails advertising new lower rates for new mining pool members. This type of behavior is likely to increase the closer the scam gets to the end of its run as current "pool" members will start to miss payments as there are no new membership fees to pass off as profits. As they do not require anything more from new members than their signup fees, these types of scams can sometimes run for a year or more. When they run out of new victims, the mining pool will fold, and the scammer will start over under a new name.

Chapter 12: Other Cryptocurrencies

Keep an eye on Ethereum

While bitcoin is definitely still at the top of the pile, it is no longer the type of hot new investment that it was a few years ago which means there are likely better alternatives when it comes to seeing the maximum amount of profit possible. No, the holder of that title is the Ethereum platform, and the currency known as ether. It has already seen about half as many transactions as bitcoin, despite only being around for a third of the time and is more firmly focused on the future with its improved interactions with smart contracts and its decentralized app platform as well.

Perhaps more importantly, if you look at the transaction chart for bitcoin then you will see that it is nothing but peaks and valleys. It's true that things tend to move in an overall positive direction, but it can hardly be called steady growth. On the contrary, the Ethereum chart shows a much more overall bullish outlook, even through the summer of 2017 when blockchain was at its current peak. It is important to keep in mind that cryptocurrencies are always going to be social constructs which means that Ethereum's robust network effects make it easier for the network, and its value, to continue to grow steadily moving forward.

This is crucial for several reasons, the first of which is that the bitcoin blockchain has already reached a point where it cannot handle any more peak usage. The bitcoin blockchain processes roughly 7 transactions each second which means that at the moment there are more than three million transactions that are sitting and waiting for the blockchain to catch up. This means that the blockchain would need to process transactions for about a week, just to catch up to where it needs to be right now. This isn't caused by any one factor so much as the fact that the blockchain is nearly a decade old and new technology has eclipsed it in virtually every way.

This, coupled with the way the platform has embraced smart contracts means that a majority of the leading developers in the blockchain space are currently in the process of shifting their products to the Ethereum blockchain. Ethereum is also capable of far more transactions per second, and the fees for each is going to be lower as well. Experts are already expecting Ethereum's user base to grow ten-fold in 2018.

It is also important to keep in mind that many of the applications that are currently in development are going to focus on making the cryptocurrency experience more user-friendly and something that the average person will be able to natively intuit. As these projects start to come online, they will cause usage rates to continue to rise and push Ethereum to the forefront of many peoples' minds when they think of blockchain or cryptocurrency technology at all.

Cryptocurrencies to watch

While bitcoin and Ethereum are at the top of the pile, there are many, many more cryptocurrencies you can explore if you are so inclined. The following list are some of the more interesting cryptocurrencies on the market today, but it is important to keep in mind that new cryptocurrencies are always coming online and the longer this book has been in the Kindle Marketplace, the less accurate the list is ultimately going to end up being. The following cryptocurrencies should be available on your favorite cryptocurrency exchange.

Litecoin: Litecoin is in many respects bitcoin 2.0, and that is clearly the impression it is trying to give off. It offers up much the same pitch as its clear inspiration except that its transaction times are much faster than what bitcoin can currently boast, cutting down on the potential for bottlenecking that is currently plaguing its namesake as well. It can process as many as five times the blocks as bitcoin can, though its methods are known to orphan blocks more frequently than bitcoin, though it also makes the potential for double-spending to occur much less likely as well. It is also known to require far less processing power when it comes to verifying litecoin transactions, as well as less when it comes to transaction fees. Payments speeds are also about four times that of what bitcoin is. There are currently about 84 million litecoins in the wild, which is about four times as many bitcoins that are left unmined. A single litecoin was worth about $40 in the summer of 2017.

Dogecoin: Dogecoin is either an example of how the internet can work together or a case of a meme going too far. It was first introduced as a joke in 2013, hence the Siba Inu dog that adorns its face. It quickly became more than that as the initial month of funding generated more than $60 million. A single dogecoin has gone on to be worth more than $1,000, and its users successfully crowdfunded a campaign to send a golden dogecoin to the moon in 2019. Currently, there are more than five billion dogecoins produced each year, and they are primarily used as a means of tipping internet comments for particularly useful or insightful content. Technically, dogecoin is also extremely on-point with a sub-60-second processing time and no cap to the number of coins that can ultimately be generated overall.

Chapter 13: Tips and Tricks

Like many things in life, getting started trading and investing in the bitcoin market is relatively straightforward, finding success, however, can be much more complicated. Keep the following in mind to ensure you get started on the right foot.

Understand it is really just like any other commodity: From a market standpoint, cryptocurrencies is just like any other type of commodity. They are all used for more than just investing, precious metals are used for jewelry, base metals are used for industrial work and bitcoin is used as a means to conduct a wide variety of specialized transactions. Like other commodities, then, it is important to choose the right bitcoin to invest in based on how the practical application side of things is doing. It does not matter what speculative investors think in the long run, only true market demand will win out in the end.

Understand mass usage is coming: Bitcoin currently has an estimated $60 billion market cap despite the fact that much of the world still has very little idea what it is exactly, just imagine what that number is going to be once things really get up and rolling. Every day, more and more people are learning about blockchain and bitcoin technology is and how it can affect their lives for the better. As this increasingly becomes the norm, more and more services are going to release to the public, and as these services become easier to use, usage rates will eventually hit mass adoption numbers. Analysts predict that this will happen around 2022 and it is at this time that the bubble surrounding bitcoin will likely burst for the last time.

The market cycle is important: The market cycle is a useful means of looking at the way all investments follow the same pattern when given a long enough timeline for doing so. The market cycle for the bitcoin, in general, is currently in the optimism phase which means that next will thrill followed by euphoria which can never be sustained which is why it is followed by anxiety, denial, fear, depression and finally panic as the price hits a point of freefall. Things then eventually right themselves and depression give way to hope, relief and optimism.

Bitcoin has already been through this cycle once before, when it bottomed out during the crash in 2014, most of the rest are still in the optimism stage, however, which means there is still plenty of opportunities to take advantage of years of investor goodwill as long as you take advantage of the market sooner than later. With the right research and a little luck, you could easily see steady returns for at least five years before you need to start worrying if your bitcoin is going to survive the impending fallout. Much like the dotcom boom of the late 90s, once the bubble bursts roughly 80 percent of all cryptocurrencies are going to go bust while the market adapts to the new major players on the scene.

Expect success in the long-term: While bitcoin saw growth of nearly $2,000 over the summer of 2017, those types of results are far from typically which means that if you want to plan on making money from bitcoin, you need to plan on doing so over the long-term. It is early days for the bitcoin market as a whole which makes the potential for exceptional deals so readily available, this will not last forever, however, so getting in soon is recommended for the best results.

However, unlike investing in other types of securities, investing in bitcoin does not involve any type of lock-in risk whatsoever as they can easily be exchanged for other types of currency at the drop of the hat instead of locking you in to a scenario where you need to rely on a third party to ensure a return on your investment. This means you can essentially use investing in bitcoin as a form of high return savings account.

Chapter 14: Bitcoin and Taxes

While, broadly speaking, you are going to treat your bitcoin-based earnings just like any other type of earning; there are also some unique tax impacts that you are going to want to keep in mind in order to ensure you are obeying the letter of the law as far as bitcoin profits are concerned. Overall, the most important thing you are going to want to keep in mind is the importance of keeping accurate records; incomplete records are going to do you the same amount of good as not keeping any records at all.

This is the case because without the proper records you will quickly find it difficult to determine just what your bitcoin-based income really is. When it comes to filing your income taxes you will find that the IRS treats bitcoins and other cryptocurrencies the same way it does property, not currency. While the specifics are more complicated, the major points to keep in mind include:

- When you dispose of your cryptocurrency you will be left with either a capital loss or gain.

- Any income that is paid via cryptocurrency is still taxable.

- The IRS sees spending bitcoin as two separate transactions, converting the cryptocurrency into dollars and then spending the resulting amount.

- Business transactions made with bitcoins are subject to standard rules regarding sales tax, reporting requirements and withholding requirements.

When it comes to cryptocurrency, the IRS has a very specific definition, it says that cryptocurrency is a digital representation of value that functions as a medium of exchange, a unit of account and/or a store of value. As such, this means it does not have the same status as legal tender, regardless of the jurisdiction. If it has an equivalent value in traditional currency or otherwise acts as a substitute for real currency then it is referred to as convertible virtual currency.

As cryptocurrency is considered property, this means that all of the general principles regarding property transactions are still going to apply. If you receive bitcoins as payment for services or goods then you must consider the current fair market value of the cryptocurrency when determining its value, based in USD on the date that it was received. Any bitcoin amounts must be listed in USD on any tax returns and you will have to include proof of what the price of bitcoin was when the forms were filed.

When it comes to the resulting capital gains that are generated when you sell your bitcoins, it is important to calculate these after each transaction where you buy or sell bitcoins, not just when you liquidate substantial parts of your holdings. As bitcoins are considered property, this means that there are three relevant points of time to consider, the point when the property was purchased, typically in exchange for cash, the period of time the property is owned and then the point in time when the property is sold.

At the end of the process, when the property is sold or otherwise disposed of several different things happen. First, you see the profit or loss that is generated from the disposal. Gains in this case are measured in the difference between the purchase price and the sale price and the tax rate in question is going to vary based on when the property was purchased and how long it was after the fact that it was then sold.

Matthew Connor

Tax tips for businesses and merchants accepting bitcoins

- Determine an exchange rate that you are going to use when it comes to valuing bitcoins, write it down and stick with it no matter what.

- Don't forget to charge sales tax, if appropriate for the item in your state as the IRS will expect you to collect it and charge you as if you did.

- If you plan on paying contractors using bitcoins make sure they file a W-9 form if you pay them more than $600 during the year. It is important that you track this amount yourself and don't count on your contractors to do it for you as some form of backup withholding may be needed.

- If you are paying your employees using bitcoin, ensure you withhold relevant taxes in USD. Net pay can then be given out in bitcoin as desired.

- Even if your business is paid exclusively via bitcoin, you will still need to pay your taxes in USD, not bitcoin. It is important to ensure you are transferring bitcoins to dollars on a regular basis to ensure you have enough on hand to meet your tax obligations when the time comes to do so.

- Regardless of how you are paid, keep your books in USD.

- Gains or losses that may come about as a result of holding bitcoins should be recorded as profits via trading gains.

- Depending on your type of business you may want to convert bitcoins to dollars immediately to prevent a loss in value.

Tax tips for private citizens

- Keep a detailed record of where you purchase and where you sell all of your bitcoins and record every sale on Form 8949.

- Take the time to determine your cost basis method early on, along with the exchange rate that you are going to primarily use as it will make your calculations easier to determine in the long run.

- Use separate wallets for long-term trading and short-term trading, keep a third wallet for personal spending if needed.

- Standard capital gains strategies will still apply. This means you will want to offset you gains with losses, time dispositions to qualify for long-term benefits and harvest losses less frequently than you harvest gains. Keep an eye on the tax rate while doing so as gains will be subject to a 3.8 percent net investment income tax.

- Depending on how frequently you mine bitcoins, and the amount you receive for doing so, it might be enough to qualify for special consideration via self-employment income. If this is the case it will be subject to both self-employment taxes and personal income taxes as well which will likely cut into your profits a good deal.

- When it comes to deductions, any investment-related expenses, investment interest, advisory or tax preparation fees as Schedule A.

Conclusion

Thank you for making it through to the end of **Mastering Bitcoin – Ultimate Beginner's Guide to Cryptocurrency Technologies - Mining, Investing and Trading in Digital Gold** let's hope it was informative and able to provide you with all of the tools you need to achieve your goals, whatever it is that they may be. Just because you've finished this book does not mean there is nothing left to learn on the topic, expanding your horizons is the only way to find the mastery you seek.

Do not forget, cryptocurrency is still in its infancy which means that, while this book is useful when it comes to helping you find your footing, you are going to need to make a habit of keeping up with the latest trends if you hope to take advantage of the next big thing. The moment you fall off of the bleeding edge is the moment you run the risk of being uninformed and missing out on a once in a lifetime opportunity.

When it comes to taking advantage of bitcoin for personal profit you will need to decide if you plan to work within the system and promote cryptocurrency directly, or if you are going to trade and invest or even mine. Regardless of which path you choose it is important to have reasonable expectations about how long it is going to take before you start seeing real results. Do not forget, the mass saturation point for cryptocurrency is still an estimated five years away which means any plans you make should be focused on the long-term for the best results. Making a play in the bitcoin market is a marathon, not a sprint, slow and steady wins the race.

Check out other Books by Matthew Connor

One Final Thing...

Did You Enjoy and Find This Book Useful?

If you did, please let me know by leaving a review on AMAZON. Reviews lets Amazon knows that I am providing quality material to my readers. Even a few words and rating would go a long way. I would like to thank you in advance for your time.

If you didn't, please shoot me an email at matthewconnor@bmccpublishing.com and let me know what you didn't like. I maybe able to change or update it.

Lastly, if you have any feedback to improve the book, please email me. In this age, this book can be a living book. It can be continuously improved by feedback provided by readers like you.

About The Author

Matthew Connor is a financial technology analyst and a self-taught computer programmer that currently lives in New York City. After graduating from Princeton University with an MS in Computer Science, Matt is currently working for a Fortune 500 company in Manhattan, NY. Matt is passionate about numbers and likes to analyze data to find trends and patterns. Having made his 1st million from investing in Bitcoin, Matt believes cryptocurrencies will revolutionize the world within the next 10 years. Therefore, he is setting out to share what he had learned so others can also get ahead start too. During his spare time, Matt enjoys hiking, reading, and cooking exotic recipes.

www.ingramcontent.com/pod-product-compliance
Lightning Source LLC
Chambersburg PA
CBHW070317230526
45470CB00002B/916